contents

S0-DYD-401

Note A glossary explaining
unfamiliar terms and ingredient
begins on page 60.

2 ground **beef** facts

Because ground beef has a greater amount of cut surface area than other meat cuts, it doesn't keep as well. Make it the last thing you buy and the first thing you put into the refrigerator when you get home.

When meat is ground in big commercial grinding machines, it becomes slightly warm and even though it is chilled immediately, it will deteriorate faster than a piece of unground meat. This is why ground beef should be cooked soon after you buy it. If you have bought it at the supermarket, take it out of its styrofoam tray, place it on a plate, cover it tightly with plastic wrap and refrigerate for no more than two days before cooking.

Freezing
Wrap ground beef tightly in plastic wrap; label with the date and freeze for up to two months. Thaw wrapped meat on a plate in the refrigerator, not on the countertop.

Browning ground beef
It is very important to stir ground beef continuously to brown it and to stop it from forming big clumps. Depending upon how much ground beef you are cooking, this can take quite a bit of time and many people find it boring and tedious. But if you do not do it, your spaghetti sauce or chili con carne or tacos will contain big lumps of meat instead of uniform small pieces that blend beautifully with the other ingredients.

Ground beef does not have to be cooked for long to become tender, especially if all the pieces have been browned and separated first. If the ground beef is very fatty, cook it in a dry pan before you cook anything else. Once the meat is browned and separate, drain off the fat, remove the meat to a plate, add a little oil to the pan and cook the onions and garlic. Then return the cooked ground beef to the pan.

Cooking thoroughly
Because ground beef has been handled more than other meat, it is more likely to harbour bacteria.

For this reason, ground beef should be cooked thoroughly. If you like your hamburgers rare, buy a piece of steak and grind it yourself just before cooking.

Home-grinding

Rump steak makes excellent ground beef, especially for hamburgers, but it needs to include a little fat, otherwise it dries out while cooking. For slower-cooked dishes, like bolognese sauce, chuck steak is very good. When home-grinding, make sure you cut out all pieces of connective tissue; even when ground, they are tough.

Most home-grinding is done in a food processor. Chop the meat into small pieces first and then add them, in batches, to the food processor. If you try to do too much at once, you'll find some of the meat purees while the rest stays in big pieces. And the longer you process, the more bruised, and therefore tough, the meat becomes. Turn the processor on and off until you reach the desired texture. Choosing coarse- or fine-ground is really a matter of taste, but if it is too fine it will become almost paste-like.

Hygiene

When making meatballs, meat loaf and hamburgers, you can't avoid using your hands. Before you handle ground beef, wash your hands and scrub your nails thoroughly with hot soapy water.

4 burgers with

mustard mayonnaise

1 lb ground beef

1/2 cup packaged seasoned stuffing mix

1/4 cup catsup

1/4 cup chopped fresh parsley

2 large onions, sliced

4 hamburger buns

8 oakleaf lettuce leaves

1 large tomato, sliced thinly

1 1/2 tablespoons stone ground mustard

1/2 cup mayonnaise

Combine beef, stuffing mix, sauce and parsley in bowl; mix well. Shape beef mixture into 4 patties. Add patties to heated, greased grill pan (or broiler or barbecue), cook until browned on both sides and cooked through. Remove from pan and cover to keep warm. Add onions to same pan (or broiler or barbecue); cook until onions are soft and browned. Remove from pan and cover to keep warm.

Split buns, place halves cut-side-down in same grill pan (or broiler or barbecue); cook until toasted lightly on cut side. Top bottom halves with lettuce, tomato, patties, combined mustard and mayonnaise, onions and tops of buns.

Freeze Uncooked patties suitable
On the table in 30 minutes

6 angel **pasta** soup
with meatballs and sage

Heat water and crumbled bouillon cubes in large pan, add carrots; simmer, covered, about 10 minutes or until carrots are tender. Add the cooked Meatballs and pasta; simmer, uncovered, for about 5 minutes or until meatballs are heated through and pasta is just tender but still firm to the bite (al dente).

Meatballs Process beef, egg, egg white, sage, parmesan, breadcrumbs, tomato, onion and garlic until well combined. Roll rounded tablespoons of mixture into balls, using damp hands. Heat oil in non stick pan; cook meatballs, shaking pan occasionally, until well browned, drain on paper towels.

4 cups water

2 beef bouillon cubes

2 medium carrots, sliced thinly

4 oz angel hair pasta

meatballs

12 oz ground beef

1 egg

1 egg white

2 tablespoons chopped fresh sage

3 tablespoons grated parmesan cheese

1/2 cup fresh breadcrumbs

1 medium tomato, chopped

1 large onion, chopped finely

5 cloves garlic, crushed

3 tablespoons vegetable oil

Freeze Meatballs suitable
Microwave Soup suitable
On the table in 30 minutes

thai beef stir-fry

in lettuce cups

2 teaspoons peanut oil

1 lb ground beef

2 teaspoons red curry paste

1 medium sweet red bell pepper, sliced

1 cup bean sprouts

4 green onions, sliced

1/3 cup coconut milk

3 tablespoons lime juice

1 1/2 tablespoons fish sauce

3 tablespoons shredded fresh mint

4 large lettuce leaves

Heat oil in wok or large pan, stir-fry beef and curry paste until browned and cooked through. Add bell pepper stir-fry 1 minute. Add sprouts, onions, milk, juice and sauce; stir-fry until hot. Stir in mint. Serve stir-fry in lettuce leaves.

On the table in 20 minutes

8 beef and bean
burritos

4 x 10-inch round flour tortillas

1 cup grated
cheddar cheese

1 teaspoon hot paprika

3/4 cup sour cream

1 1/2 tablespoons chopped
fresh cilantro

beef filling

1 1/2 tablespoons olive oil

1 lb ground beef

1 medium onion,
chopped finely

1 clove garlic, crushed

14 1/2 oz can tomatoes

1 oz package taco seasoning mix

1/2 cup water

8 3/4 oz can red kidney beans,
rinsed, drained

guacamole

1 large avocado

1 baby onion, chopped finely

2 teaspoons lemon juice

few drops Tabasco

1 small tomato, chopped finely

Divide Beef Filling among the tortillas; roll up, secure with toothpicks. Carefully place tortilla rolls on greased baking sheet; sprinkle with cheddar and paprika. Bake, uncovered, at 425°F about 10 minutes or until heated through. Serve Burritos topped with Guacamole, sour cream and cilantro.

Beef Filling Heat oil in medium pan; cook beef, stirring, until well browned. Add onion and garlic; cook, stirring, until onion is soft. Add remaining ingredients, simmer, uncovered, about 15 minutes or until mixture thickens.

Guacamole Place avocado into medium bowl, mash with fork, stir in remaining ingredients.

On the table in 30 minutes

10 herbed beef and bulgur
patties

¹/₂ cup bulgur

1¹/₂ lb ground beef

2 cloves garlic, crushed

¹/₂ cup chopped fresh parsley

1¹/₂ tablespoons dry mustard

1¹/₂ tablespoons olive oil

Place bulgur in heatproof bowl, cover with boiling water, let stand 20 minutes, drain; rinse well, drain. Combine bulgur, beef, garlic, parsley and mustard in bowl; mix well. Shape mixture into 8 patties. **Heat** oil in non stick pan; cook patties until browned both sides and cooked through.

Freeze Suitable
On the table in 30 minutes

thai-style beef and
noodles

12 oz thick fresh egg noodles

3 tablespoons peanut oil

1 lb ground beef

1 medium onion, sliced

1 medium sweet red bell pepper, sliced

3 tablespoons red curry paste

1 cup coconut milk

14 1/2 oz can baby corn, drained, halved

8 oz can water chestnuts, drained, halved

1 1/2 tablespoons fish sauce

1 lb baby bok choy, chopped

1 cup bean sprouts

3 tablespoons chopped fresh cilantro

Place noodles in heatproof bowl, cover with boiling water, let stand 1 minute; drain.
Heat half the oil in wok or large pan; stir-fry beef until well browned, remove from pan. Heat remaining oil in same pan; stir-fry onion, bell pepper and curry paste, until onion is just tender. Return beef to pan with milk, corn, water chestnuts, sauce and noodles; cook, stirring, until hot. Add bok choy, sprouts and cilantro; stir until bok choy is just wilted.

On the table in 25 minutes

12 picadillo

1 1/2 tablespoons vegetable oil

2 medium onions, chopped finely

2 cloves garlic, crushed

1 lb ground beef

1 1/2 teaspoons ground cinnamon

1/2 teaspoon ground cumin

1 medium tomato, peeled, chopped

1/3 cup raisins

1/4 cup blanched almonds, toasted, chopped

1/4 cup tomato puree

1/2 cup dry red wine

2 tablespoons honey

1/4 cup vegetable oil, extra

1 large potato, chopped

3 tablespoons chopped fresh cilantro

Heat oil in pan; cook onions and garlic, stirring, until onions are soft. Add beef; cook, stirring, until changed in color. Stir in spices, tomato, raisins and half the nuts; cook, uncovered, 3 minutes. Add puree, wine and honey; simmer, uncovered, stirring occasionally, about 5 minutes or until most of the liquid is evaporated.

Heat extra oil in separate pan, cook potato in batches, turning occasionally, until browned and tender; drain on paper towels. Add potato to beef mixture; mix gently. Serve sprinkled with cilantro and remaining nuts.

On the table in 30 minutes

gourmet beef
burgers

1¹/₂ lb ground beef

1 cup fresh breadcrumbs

3 tablespoons chopped fresh parsley

3 tablespoons sun-dried tomato paste

1¹/₂ tablespoons olive oil

4 oz mozzarella cheese, sliced thinly

¹/₄ cup mayonnaise

4 bread rolls

2 oz mixed baby lettuce leaves

1 small red onion, sliced thinly

3 tablespoons drained sliced sun-dried tomatoes in oil

Combine beef, breadcrumbs, parsley and 2 tablespoons of tomato paste in large bowl; shape mixture into 4 patties. Heat oil in pan, add patties; cook until browned both sides and cooked through. Place patties on baking sheet; top with mozzarella, broil until melted. Combine remaining tomato paste and mayonnaise in small bowl. Split bread rolls in half, toast cut sides.

Sandwich patties, mayonnaise mixture, lettuce leaves, onion and sliced tomatoes between bread rolls.

Freeze Uncooked patties suitable
On the table in 25 minutes

crostini with

olive and pimiento topping

8 slices baguette-type bread (about 3/4-inch thick)

1/2 cup olive oil

2 cloves garlic, crushed

1 1/2 cups grated mozzarella cheese

olive and pimiento topping

1 1/2 tablespoons olive oil

1 medium onion, chopped

1 clove garlic, crushed

1 1/2 lb minced beef

14 1/2 oz can tomatoes

1/4 cup dry red wine

1 teaspoon sugar

1 1/2 tablespoons tomato paste

3 x 4 oz jars pimientos, drained, sliced

1/2 cup pitted black olives, halved

Lightly brush bread on both sides with combined oil and garlic; place in single layer on baking sheet. Bake, uncovered, at 425°F about 15 minutes or until browned lightly and crisp; turn halfway through cooking. Sprinkle bread evenly with mozzarella; broil or bake until melted. Top with Olive and Pimiento Topping.
Olive and Pimiento Topping Heat oil in pan; cook onion and garlic, stirring, until onion is soft. Add beef; cook, stirring, until browned. Stir in undrained crushed tomatoes, wine, sugar, and tomato paste; simmer, uncovered, until mixture is thick. Stir in pimientos and olives.

On the table in 30 minutes

mexican-style
shepherd's pie

1 1/2 tablespoons vegetable oil

1 medium onion, chopped

2 cloves garlic, crushed

8 oz ground beef

1/2 teaspoon chili powder

2 teaspoons ground cumin

14 1/2 oz can tomatoes

1 cup water

8 3/4 oz can red kidney beans, rinsed, drained

1 1/2 tablespoons all-purpose flour

1 1/2 tablespoons water, extra

1/2 cup grated cheddar cheese

1/2 cup fresh breadcrumbs

1 teaspoon paprika

topping

4 medium potatoes

1/4 cup butter

1/4 cup milk

Grease a 6-cup heatproof dish. Heat oil in pan; cook onion, garlic, beef, chili powder and cumin, stirring, until beef is browned. Stir in undrained crushed tomatoes, water, beans and blended flour and extra water; stir over heat, until mixture boils. Simmer, uncovered, about
10 minutes or until mixture is thickened. Spoon mixture into prepared dish, gently spread with Topping; sprinkle with combined cheddar, breadcrumbs and paprika. Bake, uncovered, at 450°F about 10 minutes, or until browned lightly.

Topping Boil, steam or microwave potatoes until tender, drain.
Mash potatoes, butter and milk until smooth.

Freeze Suitable
Microwave Topping suitable
On the table in 30 minutes

18 meatballs with chili
and coconut milk

1¹/₂ lb ground beef

1 medium onion, chopped

2 cloves garlic, crushed

1 teaspoon sambal oelek

1 egg, beaten lightly

1 cup fresh breadcrumbs

vegetable oil, for deep-frying

1 medium sweet red bell pepper

13 oz can coconut cream

1¹/₂ tablespoons chopped fresh cilantro

Combine beef, onion, garlic, sambal oelek, egg and breadcrumbs in bowl; mix well. Roll rounded tablespoons of mixture into balls. Deep-fry meatballs in hot oil until well browned and cooked through; drain on paper towels.

Cut bell pepper into thin strips. Bring coconut cream to boil in pan, add bell pepper, simmer, uncovered, until just tender. Add meatballs; cook until heated through. Stir in cilantro.

Freeze Meatballs suitable
On the table in 30 minutes

red cabbage and
beef stir-fry

1 medium carrot

1¹/₂ tablespoons
vegetable oil

2 cloves garlic, crushed

2 teaspoons grated
fresh ginger

1 small onion, sliced

10 oz ground beef

1 stalk celery, sliced

¹/₄ medium red cabbage,
shredded finely

3 tablespoons soy sauce

1¹/₂ tablespoons honey

1¹/₂ tablespoons
lemon juice

Cut carrot into long, thin
strips. Heat oil in wok or
large pan; stir-fry garlic,
ginger and onion until
onion is soft. Add beef;
stir-fry until browned.
Add carrot and celery;
stir-fry until just tender.
Add cabbage; stir-fry
until wilted. Stir in
combined remaining
ingredients; cook,
stirring, until hot.

On the table in 30 minutes

beef 'n' bean

pancakes

2 teaspoons vegetable oil

1 medium onion, chopped

8 oz ground beef

1/4 teaspoon chili powder

1 teaspoon ground coriander

1 teaspoon sweet paprika

1 beef bouillon cube

14 1/2 oz can tomatoes

1/2 cup water

8 3/4 oz can red kidney beans, rinsed, drained

1/3 cup low-fat plain yogurt

pancakes

2 cups self-rising flour

1 teaspoon sugar

1 egg, beaten lightly

1 cup milk

1 cup water

Heat oil in pan; cook onion, beef and spices, stirring, until beef is browned. Stir in crumbled bouillon cube, undrained crushed tomatoes and water; simmer, uncovered, about 5 minutes or until mixture is thickened slightly. Add beans, stir until hot. Top Pancakes with beef and bean mixture and yogurt.

Pancakes Sift flour and sugar in bowl, whisk in combined remaining ingredients; whisk until smooth. Pour 1/4 cup of mixture into a heated, greased pan; cook until underside is browned. Turn and brown other side. Repeat with remaining batter to make 8 pancakes.

Freeze Suitable
Microwave Beef mixture suitable
On the table in 30 minutes

22 meatballs with tomato
sauce

1¹/₂ lb ground beef

1 cup fresh breadcrumbs

¹/₃ cup grated parmesan cheese

1 clove garlic, crushed

3 tablespoons chopped fresh parsley

3 tablespoons chopped fresh basil

2 eggs, beaten lightly

all-purpose flour

3 tablespoons vegetable oil

tomato sauce

1¹/₄ cups bottled tomato pasta sauce

1 small red bell pepper, sliced

1¹/₂ tablespoons chopped fresh basil

Combine beef, breadcrumbs, parmesan, garlic, herbs and eggs in large bowl; mix well. Shape mixture into 12 meatballs; toss meatballs in flour, shake away excess flour.

Heat oil in large non stick pan; cook meatballs until browned both sides and cooked through. Serve with Tomato Sauce.

Tomato Sauce
Combine all ingredients in medium pan, stir over heat until boiling.

Freeze Meatballs suitable
Microwave Tomato Sauce suitable
On the table in 30 minutes

parsnip cakes with

spiced ground beef

1¹/₂ tablespoons vegetable oil

1 medium onion, chopped

1 teaspoon ground turmeric

1 teaspoon garam masala

1¹/₂ teaspoons ground coriander

1 lb ground beef

14¹/₂ oz can tomato puree

¹/₂ cup water

1 beef bouillon cube

2 teaspoons sugar

1¹/₂ tablespoons chopped fresh parsley

parsnip cakes

3 large parsnips, grated coarsely

3 tablespoons all-purpose flour

2 eggs, beaten lightly

3 tablespoons vegetable oil

Heat oil in pan; cook onion and spices, stirring, until onion is soft. Add beef; cook, stirring, until well browned. Add puree, water, crumbled bouillon cube and sugar; simmer, uncovered, until mixture is thick. Spoon beef mixture over Parsnip Cakes; sprinkle with parsley.

Parsnip Cakes Combine parsnips, flour and eggs in bowl; mix well. Heat oil in non stick pan, drop ¹/₃ cups of mixture into pan, flatten slightly; cook until browned and crisp on both sides, drain on paper towels.

On the table in 30 minutes

24 omelette

spring rolls

1 lb ground beef

2 green onions, chopped

4 oz fresh baby corn, sliced

2 oz button mushrooms, sliced

3 tablespoons oyster sauce

1¹/₂ tablespoons mild sweet chili sauce

1¹/₂ tablespoons soy sauce

3 tablespoons dry sherry

6 eggs

3 tablespoons water

Cook beef in large heated oiled non stick pan, stirring, until browned and cooked through. Stir in onions, corn, mushrooms and combined sauces and sherry until heated through. Remove from pan, cover to keep warm.

Whisk eggs and water in medium bowl; pour a quarter of the egg mixture into heated oiled non stick pan. Cook, tilting pan, over medium heat until omelette is browned lightly underneath and almost set; turn, cook other side until browned lightly. Remove omelette from pan; place on plate and cover to keep warm while making three more omelettes with remaining egg mixture.

Place a quarter of the beef mixture along one edge of an omelette; roll omelette over filling, fold in sides, roll up. Repeat with remaining beef mixture and omelettes.

On the table in 30 minutes

peppered patties with
brandy sauce

2 lb ground beef

3 green onions, chopped

2 beef bouillon cubes

1 small sweet red bell pepper, chopped finely

3 tablespoons coarsely ground black pepper

1 1/2 tablespoons vegetable oil

brandy sauce

1/4 cup butter

3 tablespoons brandy

1 1/4 cups cream

1/4 cup chopped fresh parsley

Combine beef, onions, crumbled bouillon cubes and bell pepper in bowl; mix well. Shape mixture into 8 patties. Roll each patty in pepper. Heat oil in large non stick pan; cook patties until browned both sides and cooked through. Serve with Brandy Sauce.

Brandy Sauce Heat butter in pan, add brandy and cream, simmer, uncovered, about 3 minutes or until thickened slightly. Stir in parsley.

Freeze Uncooked patties suitable
Microwave Brandy Sauce suitable
On the table in 30 minutes

beef and corn
kebabs

*4 large corn
cobs, trimmed*

1 lb ground beef

1 teaspoon ground cumin

*1 teaspoon ground
coriander*

3 tablespoons honey

*1¹/₂ tablespoons
soy sauce*

2 teaspoons lemon juice

1 cup fresh breadcrumbs

*3 tablespoons chopped
fresh parsley*

cooking-oil spray

Boil, steam or microwave corn until just
tender; drain. Cut corn into 1-inch rounds.
Process remaining ingredients, except
cooking-oil spray, until combined. Shape
mixture into 16 patties. Thread corn and
patties onto 4 large skewers.
Coat with cooking-oil spray. Grill or broil
kebabs until patties are cooked through.

Freeze Uncooked patties suitable
Microwave Corn suitable
On the table in 30 minutes

28 beef and noodle omelette
with ginger sauce

1 teaspoon sesame oil

1 medium onion, chopped finely

14 oz ground beef

3 tablespoons chopped fresh cilantro

4 oz thin dried egg noodles

6 eggs, beaten lightly

1¹/₂ tablespoons peanut oil

ginger sauce

2 teaspoons cornstarch

1 cup water

1¹/₂ tablespoons white vinegar

2 teaspoons soy sauce

1¹/₂ tablespoons sugar

2 teaspoons grated fresh ginger

¹/₂ medium sweet red bell pepper, sliced thinly

2 green onions, sliced thinly

Heat sesame oil in pan; cook onion and beef, stirring, until beef is well browned. Stir in cilantro. Add noodles to pan of boiling water, boil, uncovered, until tender; drain. Rinse under cold water; drain. Chop coarsely.
Combine beef mixture, noodles and eggs in large bowl; mix well. Heat oil in large non-stick pan, pour in egg mixture, cook until omelette is browned underneath. Place pan under broiler, cook until top is set and browned. Serve with Ginger Sauce.
Ginger Sauce Blend cornstarch and a little of the water in pan, stir in remaining water, vinegar, sauce and sugar, stir over heat until sauce boils and thickens. Stir in remaining ingredients.

On the table in 30 minutes

bolognese
potatoes

4 medium potatoes

*1/3 cup grated
cheddar cheese*

*1/4 cup grated
parmesan cheese*

filling

*11/2 tablespoons
olive oil*

*1 medium onion,
chopped*

1 clove garlic, crushed

14 oz ground beef

141/2 oz can tomatoes

*3 tablespoons
tomato paste*

1 beef bouillon cube

*11/2 tablespoons
chopped fresh basil*

Boil, steam or
microwave potatoes
until tender. Cut in
half, scoop out flesh
leaving 1/2-inch shell.
Mash flesh, combine
with Filling; spoon into
shells. Place on
baking sheet, sprinkle
with cheeses; broil
until cheese has
melted.

Filling Heat oil in pan;
cook onion and garlic,
stirring, until onion is
soft. Add beef; cook,
stirring, until well
browned. Add
undrained crushed
tomatoes, tomato
paste, bouillon cube
and basil; simmer,
uncovered, about
5 minutes or until
mixture has
thickened slightly.

Microwave Potatoes
suitable
On the table in 30 minutes

mexican

beef 'n' bean pizza

1½ tablespoons vegetable oil

1 medium onion, chopped

1 lb ground beef

1 cup tomato pasta sauce

1½ tablespoons chopped fresh oregano

1 oz package taco seasoning mix

8¾ oz can corn kernels, drained

8¾ oz can red kidney beans, rinsed, drained

2 x 12-inch prepared pizza crusts

½ large red onion, sliced

1 cup grated cheddar cheese

½ cup sour cream

guacamole

2 large avocados

½ large red onion, chopped finely

1½ tablespoons lime juice

3 tablespoons sour cream

Heat oil in pan; cook onion and beef, stirring, until beef is browned. Add pasta sauce and oregano; simmer, uncovered, until mixture is thick. Stir in seasoning mix, corn and beans; mix well.

Place pizza crusts on baking sheets, spread beef mixture over crusts, top with red onion and cheddar. Bake at 500°F about 15 minutes or until browned and crisp. Serve topped with Guacamole and sour cream.

Guacamole Mash avocado until smooth; stir in remaining ingredients.

On the table in 30 minutes

quick meatballs

Satay meatballs

Kofta

Swedish meatballs

satay meatballs

1½ lb ground beef

4 green onions, chopped finely

1 cup fresh breadcrumbs

1 egg, beaten lightly

¼ cup peanut butter

¾ cup coconut cream

1 teaspoon sambal oelek

2 teaspoons soy sauce

1½ tablespoons chopped fresh cilantro

Combine beef, onion, breadcrumbs and egg in large bowl; roll rounded tablespoons of mixture into balls. Cook meatballs, in batches, in heated oiled non stick pan until browned all over and cooked through. **Combine** remaining ingredients in small pan; stir over heat, without boiling, until sauce is hot. Serve over meatballs.

kofta

1½ lb ground beef

1 small onion, chopped finely

2/3 cup packaged breadcrumbs

1 egg, beaten lightly

2 cloves garlic, crushed

1 tablespoon garam masala

1/3 cup chopped fresh mint

1 cup plain yogurt

Combine beef, onion, breadcrumbs, egg, garlic, garam masala and half the mint in large bowl; roll level tablespoons of mixture into 36 oval-shaped kofta. Thread 3 kofta on each of 12 skewers; cook skewers, in batches, on oiled heated grill pan (or broiler or barbecue), until kofta are browned all over and cooked through. Serve with combined yogurt and remaining mint.

swedish meatballs

1 1/2 lb ground beef

1 medium onion, grated

1/2 cup packaged breadcrumbs

1 egg, beaten lightly

3 tablespoons chopped fresh parsley

1/4 cup cream

1/2 cup sour cream

3 tablespoons chopped fresh dill

Combine beef, onion, breadcrumbs, egg and parsley in large bowl; roll level tablespoons of mixture into balls. Cook meatballs, in batches, in heated oiled non stick pan until browned all over and cooked through. **Combine** remaining ingredients in small pan; stir over heat until hot. Serve sauce over meatballs.

spaghetti and meatballs

1 lb ground beef

1 cup fresh breadcrumbs

1 egg, beaten lightly

1 medium onion, grated

3 tablespoons catsup

3 cups bottled tomato pasta sauce

3 tablespoons chopped fresh basil

1 lb spaghetti

Combine beef, breadcrumbs, egg, onion and tomato sauce in large bowl; roll level tablespoons of mixture into balls.

Place meatballs on greased baking sheet; bake, uncovered, at 425°F about 15 minutes or until cooked through. Heat pasta sauce and basil in large pan until boiling. Add meatballs; cook, stirring, 2 minutes. **Meanwhile**, cook spaghetti in large pan of boiling water, uncovered, until just tender; drain. Serve meatballs and sauce over spaghetti.

Below: spaghetti and meatballs

34 chili beef

and beans

Heat oil in large pan; cook onion and bell peppers, stirring, until onion is soft. Add beef, ground cumin and cumin seed; cook, stirring, until beef is well browned. Add beans, crumbled bouillon cube, tomato paste and water; cook, stirring, until hot. Serve beef mixture with corn chips and sour cream; sprinkle with chopped fresh cilantro.

1¹/₂ tablespoons vegetable oil

1 large onion, chopped

1 medium sweet red bell pepper, chopped

1 medium sweet yellow bell pepper, chopped

1 lb ground beef

¹/₂ teaspoon ground cumin

1 teaspoon cumin seed

14¹/₂ oz can pinto beans in chili sauce

1 beef bouillon cube

¹/₄ cup tomato paste

¹/₄ cup water

8 oz package corn chips

¹/₂ cup sour cream

1¹/₂ tablespoons chopped fresh cilantro

Freeze Suitable
Microwave Suitable
On the table in 30 minutes

curried beef

and tomato pasta

1¹/₂ tablespoons vegetable oil

2 medium onions, sliced

2 cloves garlic, crushed

1¹/₂ tablespoons mild curry powder

2 lb ground beef

2 x 14¹/₂ oz cans tomatoes

1¹/₄ cups bottled tomato pasta sauce

¹/₄ cup chopped fresh basil

2¹/₂ cups water

8 oz small shell pasta

Heat oil in pan; cook onions, garlic and curry powder, stirring, until onions are soft. Add beef; cook, stirring, until browned. Stir in undrained crushed tomatoes, pasta sauce, basil, water and pasta; simmer, covered, stirring occasionally, about 15 minutes or until pasta is tender.

Freeze Suitable
Microwave Suitable
On the table in 30 minutes

curried beef and lime
noodles

1 small sweet red
bell pepper

1 small sweet yellow
bell pepper

4 green onions

8 oz dried wide
rice noodles

1¹/₂ tablespoons
peanut oil

1¹/₂ lb ground beef

1 medium onion,
chopped

2 cloves garlic,
crushed

2 kaffir lime
leaves, torn

¹/₃ cup red curry paste

3 tablespoons
lime juice

3 tablespoons
fish sauce

1¹/₂ cups beef stock

2 teaspoons
cornstarch

3 tablespoons
fresh cilantro

Quarter bell peppers, remove seeds and membranes. Roast under broiler, skin side up, until skin blisters and blackens. Cover with plastic or paper for 5 minutes, peel. Slice peppers into 1/8-inch strips.

Halve green onions lengthwise; slice halves into 1/8-inch-thick strips. Place bell pepper and onion in large bowl of iced water. Cover; refrigerate 30 minutes or until strips curl.

Place noodles in large heatproof bowl, cover with boiling water, let stand until just tender; drain. Rinse well under cold water; drain.

Heat half the oil in wok or large pan; cook beef, in batches, until well browned. Remove from pan.

Heat remaining oil in same pan; stir-fry onion, garlic and lime leaves until onion is soft. Add combined curry paste, juice and sauce; stir-fry 1 minute. Add blended stock and cornstarch. Bring to boil; simmer, stirring, until thickened slightly. Return beef to pan with noodles; stir-fry until heated through. Serve topped with drained curled bell pepper, green onion strips, and cilantro.

On the table in 30 minutes

38 savory

ground beef

1 tablespoon butter

1 medium onion, chopped

1 lb ground beef

3 tablespoons all-purpose flour

1 cup water

1/2 teaspoon dried oregano

1 beef bouillon cube

1/4 cup catsup

11/2 tablespoons chopped
fresh parsley

Heat butter in pan; cook onion,
stirring, until soft. Add beef; cook,
stirring, until browned. Add flour;
cook, stirring, 1 minute. Add water,
oregano, crumbled bouillon cube
and catsup; simmer, covered,
10 minutes. Stir in parsley; mix well.
Serve savory ground beef in whole
baked potatoes topped with sour
cream, if desired.

On the table in 30 minutes

curried

ground beef

1½ tablespoons
vegetable oil

1 medium onion,
chopped

2 medium carrots,
chopped

2 lb ground beef

2 medium potatoes,
chopped

1½ tablespoons mild
curry powder

3 tablespoons
all-purpose flour

1 medium green
apple, peeled, grated

½ cup golden raisins

1 cup beef stock

2 cups water

3 tablespoons
apricot jam

Heat oil in pan; cook onion and carrots, stirring, until onion is soft. Add
beef; cook, stirring, until well browned. Stir in potatoes, curry powder and
flour; cook, stirring, 1 minute. Stir in remaining ingredients; simmer,
uncovered, about 10 minutes or until vegetables are tender and mixture is
thickened slightly.

On the table in 30 minutes

beef and
pasta bake

2 teaspoons olive oil

1 large onion, chopped

1 clove garlic, crushed

2 bacon slices, chopped finely

1 small carrot, chopped finely

1 stalk celery, chopped finely

12 oz button mushrooms, chopped

1 lb minced beef

10³/₄ oz can tomato soup

¹/₃ cup tomato paste

1 teaspoon dried oregano

6 oz spiral pasta

1 cup grated cheddar cheese

Heat oil in large pan; cook onion, garlic, bacon, carrot and celery, stirring, until carrot is just tender. Add mushrooms; cook, stirring, 2 minutes. Add beef; cook, stirring, until beef changes color. Add undiluted soup, tomato paste and oregano; simmer, covered, about 10 minutes or until mixture has thickened slightly. **Meanwhile,** cook pasta in large pan of boiling water, uncovered, until just tender; drain. Stir pasta into beef mixture; spoon into oiled deep 8-cup ovenproof dish, sprinkle with cheddar. Bake, uncovered, at 450°F about 10 minutes or until browned lightly.

On the table in 30 minutes

ground beef with

garbanzos

1 teaspoon
vegetable oil

2 cloves garlic,
crushed

1 medium onion,
chopped

1 lb ground beef

14^1/$_2$ oz can tomatoes

3 tablespoons
tomato paste

1 beef bouillon cube

1 teaspoon allspice

8^3/$_4$ oz can garbanzos,
rinsed, drained

4 oz snow peas

1^1/$_2$ tablespoons
chopped fresh parsley

Heat oil in large pan; cook garlic and onion,
stirring, until onion is soft. Add beef; cook,
stirring, until browned. Add undrained crushed
tomatoes, tomato paste, crumbled bouillon cube
and allspice; simmer, covered, until beef is
cooked. Stir in garbanzos and snow peas;
simmer, uncovered, 5 minutes. Stir in parsley.

Microwave Suitable
On the table in 25 minutes

cottage
pie nests

4 medium potatoes,
peeled, chopped

1¹/₂ tablespoons milk

1 tablespoon butter

1 egg yolk

1 tablespoon butter,
extra, melted

1¹/₂ tablespoons
vegetable oil

2 cloves garlic,
crushed

1 lb ground beef

16 oz jar tomato
pasta sauce

Boil, steam or microwave
potatoes until tender; drain.
Mash potatoes with milk and butter in
bowl until smooth; cool slightly. Stir egg
yolk into potato mixture. Spoon potato mixture into piping bag
fitted with a ¹/₂-inch star tube. Pipe four 4-inch nest shapes
onto greased baking sheet. Brush with extra butter, bake at
450°F about 20 minutes or until browned lightly.

Meanwhile, heat oil in pan; cook garlic and beef, stirring, until
browned. Add sauce; simmer, uncovered, about 10 minutes or
until thickened slightly. Spoon beef mixture into potato nests.

On the table in 30 minutes

44 minted meatballs
with hummus

Combine beef, breadcrumbs, garlic, crumbled bouillon cube, egg and mint in large bowl; mix well. Roll rounded tablespoons of mixture into balls. Heat oil in non stick pan; cook meatballs, shaking pan occasionally, until browned all over and cooked through. Serve with Hummus.

Hummus Blend or process undrained garbanzos with oil, garlic and lemon juice until almost smooth; stir in mint.

1 lb ground beef

1 cup fresh breadcrumbs

1 clove garlic, crushed

1 beef bouillon cube

1 egg, beaten lightly

3 tablespoons chopped fresh mint

3 tablespoons olive oil

hummus

8³/4 oz can garbanzos

1¹/2 tablespoons olive oil

1 clove garlic, crushed

3 tablespoons lemon juice

3 tablespoons chopped fresh mint

Freeze Uncooked meatballs suitable

On the table in 30 minutes

spaghetti
bolognese

1¹/₂ tablespoons olive oil

1 medium onion, grated

1 clove garlic, crushed

1 lb ground beef

14¹/₂ oz can tomatoes

¹/₄ cup tomato paste

¹/₄ cup water

2 beef bouillon cubes

¹/₂ teaspoon sugar

¹/₂ teaspoon dried basil

1 lb spaghetti

Freeze Sauce suitable
Microwave Pasta suitable
On the table in 30 minutes

Heat oil in pan; cook onion and garlic, stirring, until onion is soft. Add beef; cook, stirring, until browned. Add undrained crushed tomatoes, tomato paste, water, crumbled bouillon cubes, sugar and basil; simmer, covered, about 15 minutes or until sauce is thickened slightly. Meanwhile, cook pasta in large pan of boiling water, uncovered, until just tender; drain. Serve sauce over pasta.

creamy
mushroom beef

8 oz penne pasta

1 1/2 tablespoons
vegetable oil

1 medium onion,
sliced

1 clove garlic, crushed

1 lb ground beef

1 teaspoon paprika

3 tablespoons
tomato paste

8 oz can sliced
mushrooms

1/2 cup sour cream

1/4 cup water

Add pasta to large pan of boiling water, boil, uncovered, until just
tender; drain.

Heat oil in pan; cook onion, garlic and beef, stirring, until beef is
browned. Stir in paprika, tomato paste and mushrooms; simmer,
uncovered, 5 minutes. Stir in sour cream and water; stir over heat until
heated through. Serve beef mixture with pasta.

Microwave Suitable
On the table in 30 minutes

minted

meatball curry

1 lb ground beef

3 tablespoons fruit chutney

1¹/₂ tablespoons hot curry paste

1 egg, beaten lightly

1¹/₂ cups fresh breadcrumbs

3 tablespoons chopped fresh cilantro

¹/₄ cup vegetable oil

1 large onion, chopped finely

¹/₄ cup hot curry paste, extra

14¹/₂ oz can tomatoes

1¹/₂ cups water

1¹/₂ tablespoons fruit chutney, extra

3 tablespoons chopped fresh mint

On the table in 30 minutes

Combine beef, chutney, curry paste, egg, breadcrumbs and cilantro in bowl; mix well. Roll level tablespoons of mixture into balls. Heat oil in non stick pan; cook meatballs, shaking pan occasionally, until browned all over and cooked through, drain on paper towels. Reserve1¹/₂ tablespoons of oil in pan, add onion and extra curry paste; cook, stirring, until onion is soft. **Add** undrained crushed tomatoes, water, extra chutney and meatballs; simmer, uncovered, until sauce is thickened. Stir in mint.

48 mini beef and vegetable pies

1¹/₂ tablespoons vegetable oil

1 medium onion, sliced

2 cloves garlic, crushed

1¹/₂ lb ground beef

1 cup frozen mixed vegetables

2 beef bouillon cubes

1 teaspoon dried rosemary

¹/₄ cup tomato paste

3 tablespoons barbecue sauce

1 cup water

¹/₂ cup dry white wine

2 tablespoons all-purpose flour

3 tablespoons water, extra

1 sheet ready-rolled puff pastry

1¹/₂ tablespoons milk

Heat oil in pan; cook onion and garlic, stirring, until onion is soft. Add beef; cook, stirring, until browned. Add vegetables, crumbled bouillon cubes, rosemary, tomato paste, sauce, water and wine; simmer, uncovered, 2 minutes. Stir in blended flour and extra water, stir over heat until mixture boils and thickens. Spoon mixture into four 1-cup heatproof dishes.

Cut 4 rounds from pastry, large enough to cover dishes, place pastry rounds on top of dishes. Brush pastry with milk, place dishes on baking sheet. Bake at 500°F about 5 minutes or until pastry is puffed and browned.

On the table in 30 minutes

spicy beef

with noodles

2 medium carrots

2 lb thick fresh
rice noodles

3 tablespoons
peanut oil

1 1/2 lb ground beef

1 small onion,
sliced thinly

2 cloves garlic,
crushed

1/4 teaspoon five-spice
powder

1/2 cup mild sweet
chili sauce

1 lb baby bok choy,
chopped

1/4 cup hoisin sauce

3 tablespoons
soy sauce

1 1/2 tablespoons
fish sauce

3 tablespoons
chopped fresh cilantro

Using a vegetable peeler, cut carrots into long
thin strips.
Place noodles in bowl, cover with warm water,
let stand 5 minutes; drain.
Heat oil in wok or large pan; stir-fry beef, onion,
garlic and spice until beef is browned. Add chili
sauce; stir-fry until mixture is well browned.
Add carrots, noodles and remaining ingredients;
stir-fry until vegetables are just tender.

On the table in 25 minutes

50 beef
tacos

1½ tablespoons vegetable oil

1 lb ground beef

1 medium onion, chopped

1 oz package taco seasoning mix

8¾ oz can red kidney beans, rinsed, drained

⅔ cup tomato puree

12 taco shells

4 lettuce leaves, shredded

2 medium tomatoes, chopped

1 medium avocado, chopped

1½ cups grated cheddar cheese

Heat oil in pan; cook beef and onion, stirring, until beef is browned. Stir in seasoning mix, beans and puree; simmer, uncovered, about 5 minutes or until thick.

Place taco shells, upside down, on baking sheet. Bake at 375°F about 5 minutes or until crisp. Spoon beef mixture into shells; top with lettuce, tomatoes, avocado and cheese.

On the table in 20 minutes

52 tomato soup with
meatballs and pasta

1½ tablespoons olive oil

1 medium onion, chopped

2 cloves garlic, crushed

28 oz can tomatoes

2 tablespoons tomato paste

3 beef bouillon cubes

6 cups hot water

1½ tablespoons sugar

⅓ cup small elbow pasta

3 tablespoons chopped fresh basil

meatballs

1 lb ground beef

¾ cup fresh breadcrumbs

1 medium onion, chopped

1 egg yolk

1½ tablespoons chopped fresh basil

1½ tablespoons olive oil

Heat oil in large pan; cook onion and garlic, stirring, until onion is soft. Add undrained crushed tomatoes, tomato paste, crumbled bouillon cubes, water and sugar; simmer, covered,15 minutes. Stir in pasta and Meatballs; boil, uncovered, until pasta is tender. Stir in basil.
Meatballs Process beef, breadcrumbs, onion, egg yolk and basil until well combined. Roll level tablespoons of mixture into balls, using damp hands. Heat oil in non stick pan; cook meatballs, shaking pan occasionally, until browned and cooked through, drain on paper towels.

On the table in 30 minutes

spicy noodles with

beef and cashews

*12 oz thin fresh
egg noodles*

*3 tablespoons
peanut oil*

*1 teaspoon grated
fresh ginger*

1 clove garlic, crushed

*1 teaspoon
sambal oelek*

1 lb ground beef

*3 tablespoons
hoisin sauce*

*1/2 teaspoon
sesame oil*

1 beef bouillon cube

1 cup water

*2 teaspoons
cornstarch*

*3 tablespoons
soy sauce*

*3 tablespoons
chopped fresh cilantro*

*1 cup roasted unsalted
cashews*

Cook noodles in large pan of boiling water,
uncovered, until just tender; drain.
Heat oil in pan; cook ginger, garlic, sambal
oelek and beef, stirring, until beef is browned.
Stir in hoisin sauce, sesame oil, crumbled
bouillon cube, water and blended cornstarch
and soy sauce, stir over heat until mixture boils
and thickens. Stir in noodles, cilantro and
cashews; stir over heat until hot.

On the table in 25 minutes

mexican meatball

soup

1¹/₂ tablespoons
olive oil

1 medium onion,
chopped

2 cloves garlic,
crushed

1 teaspoon
sambal oelek

28 oz can tomatoes

6 cups beef stock

1¹/₂ tablespoons
chopped fresh parsley

8³/₄ oz can red kidney
beans, rinsed, drained

¹/₂ cup sour cream

2 green onions,
sliced thinly

meatballs

1 lb ground beef

2 green onions,
chopped finely

1 egg, beaten lightly

¹/₄ cup packaged
breadcrumbs

1 oz package taco
seasoning mix

1¹/₂ tablespoons
olive oil

Heat oil in pan; cook onion and garlic, stirring, until onion is soft. Add sambal oelek; cook, stirring, 1 minute. Stir in undrained crushed tomatoes and stock; simmer, covered, 15 minutes. Add parsley, beans and cooked Meatballs to pan, simmer, covered, until meatballs are cooked through. Serve topped with sour cream and green onions.
Meatballs Combine all ingredients, except oil, in bowl; mix well. Roll level tablespoons of mixture into balls. Heat oil in large non stick pan; cook meatballs, shaking pan occasionally, until browned all over, drain on paper towels.

Freeze Meatballs and soup, separately
Microwave Soup suitable
On the table in 30 minutes

pasta with mushrooms

and basil

1¹/₂ tablespoons olive oil

1 medium onion, sliced

3 cloves garlic, crushed

1 lb ground beef

8 oz button mushrooms, sliced

¹/₂ cup dry white wine

28 oz can tomatoes

1 beef bouillon cube

¹/₄ cup shredded fresh basil

3 tablespoons chopped fresh chives

8 oz spiral pasta

Heat oil in pan; cook onion and garlic, stirring, until onion is soft. Add beef; cook, stirring, until well browned. Add mushrooms; cook, stirring, until mushrooms are soft. Stir in wine, undrained crushed tomatoes and crumbled bouillon cube; simmer, uncovered, until thickened slightly. Stir in herbs.

Freeze Suitable
Microwave Suitable
On the table in 30 minutes

Meanwhile, cook pasta in large pan of boiling water, uncovered, until just tender; drain. Stir sauce together with pasta.

fried noodles

with garlic beef

6 oz rice vermicelli noodles

3 tablespoons peanut oil

1 lb ground beef

1½ tablespoons mild sweet chili sauce

1½ tablespoons black bean sauce

3 tablespoons soy sauce

3 cloves garlic, crushed

1 medium carrot, sliced thinly

1½ cups chopped broccoli

4 oz snow peas

3 tablespoons soy sauce, extra

Place noodles in heatproof bowl, cover with boiling water, let stand 5 minutes; drain well.
Heat oil in pan; cook beef, stirring, until well browned. Add sauces, garlic, carrot, broccoli and snow peas; cook, stirring, until vegetables are just tender. Add noodles and extra soy sauce; stir over heat until hot.

On the table in 25 minutes

58 beef risotto with
sun-dried tomatoes

Heat butter in pan; cook onion and garlic, stirring, until onion is soft. Add beef; cook, stirring, until beef is browned. Stir in stock, undrained crushed tomatoes, tomato paste and rice. Simmer, covered, about 20 minutes, or until almost all the liquid is absorbed, stirring, occasionally. **Add** mushrooms and zucchini; cook, covered, until rice and vegetables are tender. Remove from heat, stir in sun-dried tomatoes, half the parmesan and basil. Serve sprinkled with remaining parmesan flakes.

$^1/_4$ cup butter

1 small onion, chopped finely

2 cloves garlic, crushed

1 lb ground beef

1$^1/_2$ cups beef stock

14$^1/_2$ oz can tomatoes

$^1/_4$ cup tomato paste

1 cup white short-grain rice

4 oz button mushrooms, sliced

2 small zucchini, sliced

$^1/_4$ cup drained sun-dried tomatoes in oil, sliced

$^1/_2$ cup parmesan cheese flakes

$^1/_4$ cup shredded fresh basil

On the table in 30 minutes

kidney bean
meat loaves

1 medium onion, chopped finely

1 lb ground beef

2 teaspoons dried Italian seasoning

1 cup fresh breadcrumbs

1/4 cup tomato paste

8 3/4 oz can red kidney beans, rinsed, drained

1 egg, beaten lightly

1 teaspoon ground cumin

3 tablespoons chopped fresh chives

Lightly grease four 1-cup ovenproof dishes. Combine ingredients in large bowl; mix well. Press mixture evenly into prepared dishes. **Bake**, uncovered, at 375°F about 20 minutes or until cooked through. Let stand 2 minutes before turning out.

On the table in 30 minutes

glossary

allspice berry resembles an oversized reddish brown peppercorn; available whole or ground. Tastes like a mixture of cinnamon, clove and nutmeg.

arugula a green salad leaf with a nutty, peppery taste.

barbecue sauce a spicy, tomato-based sauce used to marinate or baste, or as an accompaniment.

beef, ground

chuck: cheapest grade; contains 30% fat.

lean: middle grade; contains about 20% fat.

sirloin or extra lean: leanest grade; contains about 15% fat.

bell pepper available in green, yellow or red.

black bean sauce a Chinese sauce made from fermented soy beans, water and wheat flour.

breadcrumbs

fresh: one- or two-day-old bread made into crumbs by grating or processing.

packaged: fine-textured, crunchy, purchased white breadcrumbs.

bulgur cracked wheat; used in Middle-eastern dishes such as kibbeh and taboulleh.

butter 8 tablespooons or $1/2$ cup is equal to 1 stick butter.

cilantro also known as Chinese parsley; bright-green-leafed herb with pungent flavor. Often stirred into a dish just before serving.

coconut

cream: available in cans; made from coconut and water.

milk: pure, unsweetened coconut milk available in cans from supermarkets.

cornstarch derived from corn; used as a thickening agent in cooking.

fish sauce also called nam pla or nuoc nam; made from pulverised salted fermented fish. Available in Asian markets and major supermarkets.

five-spice powder a Chinese spice blend of ground cinnamon, cloves, star anise, Szechuan pepper and fennel seeds.

garbanzo beans also called chickpeas; an irregularly round, sandy-colored legume used extensively in Mediterranean cooking.

garam masala a powdered blend of Indian spices, based on cardamom, cinnamon, clove, coriander, and cumin. Sometimes chili is added.

ginger, fresh also known as green or root ginger; the root of a tropical plant.

gravy mix a flour-based product used to thicken and add flavor to sauces, casseroles and soups.

hoisin sauce a thick, sweet and spicy Chinese paste made from salted fermented soy beans, onions and garlic.

hummus a smooth Middle-eastern dip made of garbanzos, tahini, garlic and lemon juice.

kaffir lime leaves aromatic leaves of a small citrus tree bearing a wrinkled-skinned yellow-green fruit; use fresh or dried. Available in Asian markets and majpr supermarkets.

mixed baby lettuce leaves also known as mesclun, salad mix or gourmet salad mix; a mixture of assorted young lettuce and other green leaves.

oil

cooking oil spray: vegetable oil in an aerosol can, available in supermarkets.

olive: a mono-unsaturated oil, made from the pressing of olives; especially good for everyday cooking and in salad dressings. Light describes the mild flavour, not the fat levels.

peanut: pressed from ground peanuts; commonly used in Asian cooking because of its high smoke point.

sesame: also known as dark sesame oil; made from roasted, crushed, white sesame seeds; a flavoring rather than a cooking medium.

vegetable: any of a number of oils sourced from plants rather than animal fats.

onion

green: also known as scallion or (incorrectly) shallot; an immature onion picked before the bulb has formed, having a long, green edible stalk.

red: also known as Spanish, red Spanish or Bermuda onion; a sweet-flavored, large, purple-red onion.

oyster sauce a thick dark-brown sauce made from oysters, salt and soy sauce. Available in Asian markets and major supermarkets.

paprika ground dried red bell pepper; available sweet or hot.

pimientos canned or bottled red peppers.

pine nuts also known as pignoli. Small cream-coloured kernels.

puff pastry, ready rolled packaged sheets of frozen puff pastry, available from supermarkets.

soy sauce made from fermented soy beans. Several varieties are available

in most supermarkets and Asian markets.

taco seasoning mix a packaged seasoning mix made from oregano, cumin, chilies and other spices.

tomato

catsup: a sauce based on tomatoes, vinegar, sugar and various spices.

paste: a concentrated tomato puree used to flavour soups, stews and sauces.

puree: canned pureed tomatoes (not a concentrate); use fresh, peeled, pureed tomatoes as a substitute.

pasta sauce: ready-to-use bottled sauce, made from tomatoes, onions, celery, peppers and seasonings.

index

mini books
maxi results

- healthy eating
- make it tonight
- sweet and simple

on sale at selected retailers supermarkets

© ACP Publishing Pty Limited 1998
© Cole Publishing Group, Inc. 1999

Make it tonight: Hamburger and more
ISBN 1-56426-206-5
Library of Congress Cataloging-in-Process
Printed in Hong Kong
F E D C B
4 3 2 1 0 9

Cole Publishing Group, Inc. is not responsible for
unsolicited manuscripts, photographs or illustrations.
Cole Publishing Group, Inc.
13750 Arnold Drive
P.O. 2199
Glen Ellen, CA 95442-2199 USA
Voice   (707) 939-9400
Fax   (707) 939-9496
www.coleshomelibrary.com

Cole's Home Library Cookbooks

Distributed to the book trade by:
ACCESS Publishers Network, Grawn, MI 49637

Cole books are available for quantity purchase for sales
promotions, presentations, fund-raising or educational use.
For further information on Cole books, contact the publisher.